Eight Steps *to a Successful* Release

A strategy for moving from incarceration to freedom.

by
Julia G. Chavez

Copyright ©2020 Julia G. Chavez

All rights reserved. No part of this publication may be reproduced, distributed, or transmitted in any form or by any means, including photocopying, recording, or other electronic or mechanical methods, without the prior written permission of the publisher, except in the case of brief quotations embodied in critical reviews and certain other noncommercial uses permitted by copyright law.

The Authorized King James Version of the bible is in the Public Domain.

Scriptures taken from the Holy Bible, New International Version®, NIV®. Copyright © 1973, 1978, 1984, 2011 by Biblica, Inc.™ Used by permission of Zondervan. All rights reserved worldwide. www.zondervan.com The "NIV" and "New International Version" are trademarks registered in the United States Patent and Trademark Office by Biblica, Inc.™

ISBN-978-1-951300-08-1

Liberation's Publishing – West Point - Mississippi

Eight Steps
to a Successful
Release

A strategy for moving from incarceration to freedom.

by
Julia G. Chavez

Julia G. Chavez

Table of Content

Introduction 7

1 Step One 11

2 Step Two 15

3 Step Three 17

4 Step four 19

5 Step Five 23

6 Step Six 25

7 Step Seven 27

8 Step Eight 31

In Closing 33

Eight Steps to a Successful Release!

Introduction

Learning is the beginning of wealth. Learning is the beginning of health. Learning is the beginning of spirituality. Searching and learning is where the miracle process begins.

-Johnny Gonzales

I honestly believe that my cousin fully understood the power of knowledge. Some people say if you know better, you do better. But what if you just don't know what better is? What if your poor choices come from a background or a cycle of bad choices. What is your home-training? Is it from an alcoholic or addicted mother or father? What about an abusive father or both? What about parents that were never taught to make good decisions? What if all you knew ended you up in one of the saddest, loneliest, most depressing places on earth?

These are thing I questioned God about back in 2014. I was in prison, and I received a visit from my mother. She made a special visit to tell me one of the most painful things I had to endure. She came by, and I was surprised. No one ever came to visit me. I sat down and looked up at her as she picked up the phone. She was standing, so I said mom, "sit down." She replied with, "No. I just came to tell you that I'm not visiting you anymore."

My heart stopped, and it seemed as if I was in another

realm. I heard her speaking, but it seemed to be coming from another place.

"Since you love being her so much, you stay here."

"Did I have a choice?" I thought to myself while still processing her message.

"I'm not bringing your kids. I'm not putting money on your book, or on the phone."

I kept agonizing. Each phrase was like a blow to my heart.

"I'm not going to ask your kids to write to you. This is the last time I will ever try to bring them to see you."

I said, "Mom, I'm going to do better."

"That's what you always say, but since you love this place so much, more than being home with your kids, I'm done. I'm tired of having to comfort them when they cry for you.

"Mom!"

Her words were too hard to bear. She took the knife in my heart and twisted it with anger, pain, and disappointment. I couldn't get a word out. With pain in her eyes and voice shrieking all while trying not to shed a tear, she continued on, "All three of your kids are here. Only two of them are allowed. I'm not going to bring two and leave one out there alone crying. All three of them are out there crying for you. You hurt them more than anyone could. I'm done." She slammed the phone down and walked away.

This has to be a dream.

As my heart began to capture the pain that came in the form of her words I sat there, dumfounded. I tried to interject but couldn't. She said what she said and was gone. In that moment I couldn't speak. I couldn't cry. I couldn't fight. All I could do was go back to my cell, which is what I did and listened to the door slam shut behind me. This time the sound was different. It was awful and heavy. The sound of it seemed to enrage me.

I hated the fact that I was in there. I hated that I had made so many bad decisions. I hated the steps I had taken to land me there. I hated how my mother cold heartedly shut me out. I didn't like being there! I hated knowing my kids were suffering because of me. As I sat there huffing and puffing with anger, I couldn't help but notice that the sun was shinning into my cell. It was not ordinary. There was something about that light.

In one of my darkest hours light shinned on me. Lord knows I had accumulated years of darkness, but there was something about the way the sun shinned on me in that cell. I began to talk to God. I confessed that I was tired. I needed help. I could only imagine being clean in a nice home with my kids. I could only imagine a place where we were safe and not worrying about bills or food. I could almost see them laughing, running, and playing. I even imagined myself calling out to them, "Get your shower. Where're your clothes for tomorrow." Oh, the joy of that becoming true for me. That was the day of my encounter with God. Blessed be the day of my brokenness.

Some days later, I heard girls saying they were going to church. I went with them. My ears were like satellites ready to receive. I didn't know what was going to happen or what to expect. The only thing I did know was that I needed Jesus. I remember those ladies. I remember the first time I heard their testimonies. That night I received my first dose of hope. I believed God could change me like He changed them. He did!

My hope now is that my testimony will have the same effect on you! Be blessed, my beloved brothers and sisters.

-Julia

1 Step One

Be aware of changes. The U.S. Department of health states, *"some inmates may come to depend heavily on institutional decisionmakers to make choices for them and to rely on the structure and schedule of the institution to organize their daily routine. Although it rarely occurs to such a degree, some people do lose the capacity to initiate behavior on their own and the judgment to make decisions for themselves. Indeed, in extreme cases, profoundly institutionalized persons may become extremely uncomfortable when and if their previous freedom and autonomy is returned.*[1] You must understand that even though you've been locked up, the world, people, and places have changed. It's almost as if time has stood still for you. These things may have changed a little or a lot. You must also consider that you have changed too.

Philippians 4:7 says, "and the peace of God which surpassed all understanding shall keep your hearts and minds through Christ Jesus." (KJV)

Proverbs 4:7says, "Wisdom is the principal thing; therefore, get wisdom: and with all thy getting get understanding." (KJV)

---

[1] https://aspe.hhs.gov/basic-report/psychological-impact-incarceration-implications-post-prison-adjustment

Understanding the reason behind the things going on in your life is key; it's very important. You have to consider things that landed you were you are. There is no judging here, just taking into an account of things.

We have to be aware, as I'm sure by now you are, that behind every decision good or bad there is a consequence. There is a reaction from the decisions we make. They not only affect us. They also affect the ones around us. You must always be conscious of that. Don't think on impulse. That was my biggest problem. Acting without processing the fact that things aren't how they used to be. I'm not how I used to be. Forgetting could land me right back in that booking room. The decisions you make from here on out will determine the rest of your life. Every day you wake up is an opportunity to be better than you were the day before.

Here is where you will allow God to teach you and help you learn from the good and the bad. It may seem crazy, but there is a lesson in the good and bad. Now is a good time to question God concerning your steps. It's okay to ask why. Set aside all judgement. Proverbs 3:5-6 says, *"Trust in the LORD with all thine heart; and lean not unto thine own understanding. 6-In all thy ways acknowledge him, and he shall direct thy paths."* (KJV)

God is so amazing that He will help you understand why you made the mistakes you did. He will also let you know what factors played into your life choices. God is perfect. He judges righteously. He does not condemn. He helps us to understand ourselves better. Once we understand ourselves, the why and how become easier for us to understand. We understand why we are the way we are, and why we've done the things we've done.

Eight Steps to a Successful Release!

2 Step Two

Be Aware of depression. Depression after incarceration is very common. Depression most likely begins while incarcerated and then follows you once you're released. It follows because now you have to adjust to living in the world again. We went from not paying bills for basic things like shelter, utilities, food, and even a bed to sleep on, to having to supply all of these things ourselves. To add to it you're released into society, some with skills to work some with little to none, and homeless. Its hard to start over.

Be strong. You can do it. Prepare yourself mentally. There are people out there who care, but when you find them take the opportunity and use it to your maximum capability. Depression is like prison. It can either make you or break you. When the opportunity comes along you take it, and you go with it. Your life and future depend on it. No excuses. You're stronger than depression because depression is a thing of this world. If God is in you and with you, then greater is He that is in you than he that is the world, amen.

It's found that *"Depression was the most prevalent mental health condition reported by inmates, followed by mania, anxiety, and posttraumatic stress disorder."*[2] The

---

[2] https://www.ncbi.nlm.nih.gov/pmc/articles/PMC4232131/#:~:text=Depression%20was%20the%20most%20prevalent,among%20prisoners%20in%20state%20institutions.

frustration of finding a job that provides for your family alone, makes you want to give up. There are ways to fight this.

Start each day with a goal. It doesn't matter how small. Just set a goal. Having a vison before you will help you to stay focused. Once a goal is reached, celebrate your success. Applaud yourself for having done the thing you set out to do. This is the beginning of you regaining your faith in yourself. Prison took that away from you. You weren't able to make simple decisions like what time to go to sleep, what time to eat. Praise God for your freedom and you reclaiming your freedom.

Be proud of everything you accomplish. It could be paying your bills on time. Securing a place to rent. Getting your first ride. These are great accomplishments, and they set you on your path to more freedom. Applaud yourself for wanting to take the high road, the legal road to success.

Isaiah 43:1 says, *"Fear not: for I have redeemed thee, I have called thee by thy name; thou art mine." (KJV)* God commands us to not fear or worry. "Fear" is spoken of over 500 times in the KJV Most likely because the enemy uses fear to decrease our hope and limit our victories.

3 Step Three

Communicate Frustration. We all find ourselves under a lot of stress while adjusting to life after being locked up. We must become accountable for our past actions. We are forced to realize the consequences behind our mistakes. You have to vent your frustrations. You must find someone who will listen to you and encourage you while you are encouraging yourself. Don't give up! Galatians 6:9 tells us *"Let us not become weary in doing good, for at the proper time we will reap a harvest if we do not give up."* (NIV) It is so easy to get frustrated when you're trying to follow that narrow path. You can't seem to receive the support, or even the encouragement you need to keep you there.

Stay calm and be the strong person you know you can be and keep going. Write it down. Bite your tongue. Learn not to react to everything people say to or towards you in the heat of the moment. Retrain your mind. This could be one of the greatest lifesaving assets you can develop within yourself.

When someone upsets you react in a healthy manner. Sometimes we get frustrated simply because we do not fully understand what is going on. We're so used to being lied to or misused from past trauma. It tells us in proverbs 4:7 *in ALL thy getting get an understanding* (KJV) So, before you lash out in frustration get a clear understanding.

If you find yourself constantly letting frustration land

you back into positions that put you at risk of going back to jail, evaluate yourself. Ask yourself if this is really worth my life in jail? Is this really the cycle I want to endure for the rest of my life? We all know the definition of insanity. It is doing the same thing over and over and expecting a different outcome.

My beloved people doing life in prison we know that breaking the cycle of incarceration must also include unlocking the prison of your mind. If you're reading this, thank you for the support. I know your heart is for people. This system is like a revolving door, people coming through day in and day out. Depression sets in. Just know that there is a God that sits high and looks low. He has not left you, and he will continue this journey with you.

4 Step four

Manage Anger. According to the Mayo Clinic, *anger management is defined as the process of learning to recognize signs that you're becoming angry and taking action to calm down and deal with the situation in a productive way. Anger management doesn't try to keep you from being angry or encourage you to hold it in. Anger is a normal healthy emotion when you know how to express it appropriately*-[3] Learning to cope with situations that make us angry is truly a virtue. Unhealthy anger makes every situation worst, obviously. We must learn to manage stressful situations. Step back and be quiet.

Ephesians 4:6 says, *"in your anger do not sin" [a]: Do not let the sun go down while you are still angry." The problems come with what we do with anger when we feel it. We must learn to experience the anger and move on from it."* (NIV)

Anger can go right along with frustration. Frustration tends to bring on anger. What happens when we can't control a situation that we've been hoping we could change? We put our guard up to keep our emotions from showing and prevent us from showing weakness. We use anger as a guard, as our wall to show that we are bigger than the crying. We have

---

[3]https://www.mayoclinic.org/tests-procedures/anger-management/about/pac-20385186

been internally disappointed or frustrated by rejection of something we hoped would fall in our favor. We use those emotions but are hurt afterwards. Sometimes in the midst of our anger we may even become violent. We use violence as a defense. We want people to know that we are a force to be reckoned with. We refuse to allow people to take us for weak. We have created a wall around the healthy emotions, that still lie deep within.

We've just caked up so much over the healthy emotions to prevent you from getting hurt. It's a form of survival. The crazy part is that all along we're not really angry. We reacted angrily because we were hurt by a situation that was out of our control. It was a situation that was a total miscommunication. It led us to be angry, which in turn led us to lash out in violence. We had no idea how to control our emotions. We were never taught how to use our emotions in a healthy way.

We've been used to being raised in toxic environments. We lived in an atmosphere or society that told us we had to fight, kill, or be killed. For some people you had a great life. You just may have used anger, because you were used to getting what you wanted when you wanted. When it didn't happen for you, it led you to irrational thinking and behavior.

Always consider these words. Allow it to take shape into the tablets of your mind, heart, and soul. Romans 12:2 *be transformed by the renewing of your mind.* (KJV) Put aside to time to read the entire twelfth chapter of Romans. If you don't get anything else, be transformed by the renewing of your mind, that you may prove what is good, and acceptable will of God. Anger took me to places I couldn't get myself out of. Anger is a big one for me even today. I stay transparent on this. My freedom depends on it.

Some days anger consumes me. I know even with all that I have accomplished and worked so hard for; people still look at me like I'm just that person from the gutter selling dope in prostitution. Then anger builds up. As I begin to look back over my life. I remember myself as the child sleeping on piles of dirty clothes, because they were more comfortable and smelled better than the urine-soaked mattress. Some of you can relate, but some of you won't. That's where my anger started. It started from my broken childhood.

It started with my dad going to prison. I watched him bring home black garbage bags of stinky leaves that he would smoke. I watch him go away for ten years flat. I was eight when I became a mother, but some people won't catch that though. The downward spiral started with a blow.

I began to look at me how I used to be, angry and defensive. People act like they just don't know how far I've come. I began to talk myself down out of the anger and begin to see myself how God sees me. I think of my kids, my husband, my mission. I'm on a mission and negative painful conversations about me cannot hinder me. I refuse to give anyone the pleasure of seeing me lose it all because of their opinion of me. From this day forth, you carry the same mentality.

My mother couldn't handle my father going to prison. She started drinking heavily. My dad was very physically abusive to my mom and us. But I would rather take the beatings everyday than for him to have left us. As a child before my dad went to prison, I was a spoiled cry baby. I was happy loving, helpful. I remember I always wanted to help. I was afraid of everything. My older brother and my uncle were my heroes, still are. After dad went to prison, I couldn't be scared. I had to be strong. Mom was hardly there anymore. It was just my two brothers and sisters.

By the time I was eleven, my heart was stone cold. My anger was rage. Resentment tormented my soul. Life had made me bitter. The cards I had been dealt couldn't be thrown back in. I just had to sit back and play out this garbage hand I was given. When I look back now, it's kind of like getting on the scoreboard when the other team was going 10, but you snuck on in there and set them back.

…

I'll be the first to tell you if you have anger issues and a probation officer or case manager, therapist, friend, family member anyone you trust, let them help. You can even use a computer in the free world. Go to the search bar, and search for anger management classes or therapy. You can even do some self-help coping skills. Do it. It may save your life, or someone else's life. It will surely help keep you out of incarceration. Do some soul searching and find the root of your anger. Work on it. Its life changing.

5 Step Five

Deal with Rejection Positively. Rejection will come in many forms. For instance, the first few months after your release, family, friends, former employers may reject you. You must be patient with them. They are also adjusting.

It's hard to stay encouraged when doors continue to be shut in our face. Its hard to stay encouraged when you keep hitting dead end roads. It seems as though no matter how much good we're trying to do; bad things seem to come our way. No matter how hard we try people will not take into consideration how much we've changed.

Let me share something that may seem harsh. This isn't for everyone, but this is for someone. Take it as you will. Sometimes the doors keep shutting, and people are not helping you. It may seem like these opportunities are not meant to be. You have to fight harder. There may be something you've done before, but it is harder to do now. This time you're going to a place without a bridge because you burned it down on your way out. Now you're trying to go back. The bridge is no longer there. The place is still there, but now you've got to figure out a way to get there without that bridge. No worries beloved, there are other ways to get there if it be the Lords will. There are other destinations if that be the lords will. Jeremiah 29:11 *For I know the plans I have for you, declares the lord plans to prosper you and not to harm you plans to give you hope and* *a futur*e (NIV)

It's important that we stay encouraged and trust the process. Keep the mindset that "God's will be done in my life." When the door shuts say, "I trust you Lord." You have to constantly speak to your circumstances and situations. If you've never had a personal relationship with God or a higher power, then get a journal, a counselor, a mentor, a therapist, or just plain old peer support. There are services out there to help you.

You have to constantly tell yourself in those moments when you feel alone that there is someone out there that cares. They are advocating for you to succeed. They believe in you. You have to believe in yourself too. No matter what happens, you can do anything you set your mind to. It doesn't matter what you've done or been through. You can succeed. I mean look at this wretch typing these very words.

6 Step Six

Resist Negative Influences. When you are released, you'll run into external pressure to gain acceptance. Surround yourself with people who are encouraging. The best way to deal with negative influences is to be aware of them. Stay to yourself as you work on yourself. This will help you stay focused. The more you connect to groups from your past, the more you push away your goals.

Learn to be content in being yourself. This will teach you how to put your needs and desires first. Stay connected with positive groups. Don't shut away from the world. Just make better choices. 2 Corinthians 5:17 says, *"Therefore, if anyone is in Christ, the new creation has come: [a] The old has gone, the new is here"* (NIV)

One of the hardest things is separating from the ones we call family. Family can be toxic for our growth. They can be one of our biggest negative influences believe it or not. In many ways, family will continue to lead you to stay dependent. This can be in the form of doing everything for you. That hinders your own personal growth. Being independent brings such powerful encouragement and belief in yourself. When you are the captain of your own ship, you choose which way your life goes.

In my case, my choices were completely opposite my family's choices. They wouldn't help me even if they could. I refused to take a step towards the bucket to be pulled in by the crabs. Nobody is going to love you like you love you. There is only one you, so take care of you. You have a divine purpose in this life. It might not be what you think, but it surely doesn't consist of clubbing, gambling, selling dope or anything else in between. That life can get crazy really quick. Your freedom and your life depend on who you surround yourself with.

You are what you hang around. If you're no longer that thing, then why are you there in the first place. Not every invitation needs to be accepted. Life does get extremely lonely and boring, but wouldn't you much rather be lonely and bored than to be in bad company of people who could lead you right back to that booking room.

7 Step Seven

Combat Addiction. Addiction comes in many forms, drugs, alcohol, people, places, things, money. We cannot get into combat alone. We need to share our weaknesses with our close family and friends. Be bold. Don't rely on anyone of these things when it comes to your recovery. There is help out there. Push yourself to get it. 1 Timothy 4:12 says, *"Don't let anyone look down on you because you are young, but set an example for the believers in speech, in conduct, in love, in faith and in purity."* (NIV) I love that scripture, and I wish I would have taken heed or even known it when I was younger.

My addiction started at a young age. I hated my life, and I loved the high that drugs gave me. It helped me stop feeling anything in my life. It was one of those selfish and suicide persons. I was killing myself slowly and killing my family in the process. My kids suffered, and I was all they had.

Thirty-seven percent of people returning back to jail are arrested for a new crime within three years. According to the nation institute of drug abuse sixty-five percent of American prison or jail population have what they call an SUD substance use disorder. Twenty percent of people incarcerated in America not considered SUD, were still under the influence when they committed their crime.

Did you know studies show that some opioid users tend to overdose upon release because their tolerance level has decreased? Their tolerance has decreased, but they use the same amount of drugs they used before they were incarcerated.

During Jail ministry I've seen the revolving door inmates go through for drug use. It was this way for me. I've had ladies tell me, "Mrs. Julia when I get out, I'm going to leave the alcohol/dope alone, and be better. I'm going to get my kids back. I'm going to work and leave that person alone. I'm going to move on with my life and do and be better." I've heard so many hopeful things. Some have gotten out and stayed out for a while. Some got out, went to treatment, and are doing great. Some got out went and back into the system and are serving sentences in prison. Some I've gone to their funeral and given my condolences to their mothers and young children. Some got out and just decided they never wanted to go back, so they did what they had to do to stay out.

I get calls about help for treatment, and I do my best to get that help set up. I believe it helps. It works if you work it. I just know in my heart, until a person has made that decision to be sick and tired of being sick and tired, it will not happen. Prison stops being a revolving door once you want it to.

You may ask why I call things out as I see it? Because when you call it out, it loses power.

I get 3 kinds of people who want help

1.) The one who wants to beat the system. Try to use it to stay out of jail or prison or to keep their kids. These

are the ones who care about recovery.
2.) The one who wants treatment and to be sober, but they think they can quit on their own. Usually, they go into a relapse for lack of support. They refuse treatment and find a problem with every solution. They want help but aren't willing to go all in for their recovery. They want recovery to work around their desires and wants
3.) The one who is willing to do whatever it takes. The one who takes the humble narrow road to break the cycle that has crippled their life. The one who seeks help from positive people and fight with all that is in them to recover.

I'm sure there are more numbers to go there, but those are the ones that I've come across on my journey. I encourage you to be the third person.

Eight Steps to a Successful Release!

8 Step Eight

Be Innovative. Merriam Webster defines innovation as, *1) a new idea, method, or device. 2) the introduction of something new*[4]. We live in a society that is constantly looking for new and better ideas to make things easier. They can become easier to access, use or accomplish. It's important that we tune our minds into being open for new ideas.

Old things have passed away, and you have become new. People say the definition of insanity is doing the same thing over and over and expecting a different outcome. As you begin to seek a better outcome from your decisions be sure to utilize all available materials and tools to help you succeed. Keep up with what's working and what's not.

Learn the trends and use better judgement in deciding what will help you prosper or take a loss. For example, if you paint, keep up with tools that make your art more remarkable. Invest in yourself to prosper yourself. Remember you can't help anyone if you can't help yourself. If you can't help yourself let someone help you.

Let the former you be your testimony. Let your setbacks and failures be the reason you keep pressing forward. Let the pain be the fuel to your success. Even those in the free world

---

[4] https://www.merriam-webster.com/dictionary/innovation

are in prison within their minds. Being in prison and finding peace with God and myself was the freest I ever felt. My prayer is that you may find a joy that surpasses all understanding. Innovate your way of coping. Try new things with the newfound you. Search within yourself to see that you are good. You can and you will. Set your heart and mind to do so.

In Closing

Being physically released from incarceration is not the same as being released mentally and spiritually. We must understand that once our feet touch the earth, the world, people, and places have changed. Do not let this hinder the journey to enter a place of peace and positivity. Look for guidance from the following scripture:

Jeremiah 29:11 *for I know the plans I have for you declares the lord, plans to prosper you, and not harm you, plans to give you hope and a future (NIV)*

Truly I give honor to God. I praise Him for the things that he has done and the things He will do. He is not done with me yet. I'll be the first to tell you that the journey is not easy. I'm still seeking God to help me on a daily basis. Everyday is a chance I have to be better than I was the day before.

We just keep it moving. We keep moving forward and giving life our best. Every trial has a lesson. Learn from it and move on. Don't dwell on it; just keep it moving. Don't stay stuck on your mistake. We all make them. Stay strong and be of good courage.

Eight Steps to a Successful Release!